USING THIS BOOK

*One of the best ways of helping children to learn to read is by reading stories to them and with them. This way they learn what **reading** is, and they will gradually come to recognise many words, and begin to read for themselves.*

First, grown-ups read the story on the left-hand pages aloud to the child.

You can reread the story as often as the child enjoys hearing it. Talk about the pictures as you go.

Later the child will read the words under the pictures on the right-hand page.

The pages at the back of the book will give you some ideas for helping your child to read.

British Library Cataloguing in Publication Data
McCullagh, Sheila K.
    Tessa and the magician.—(Puddle Lane. Series no. 855. Stage 1; v. 2)
    I. Title   II. Lobban, John   III. Series
    428.6   PR6063.A165/
    ISBN 0-7214-0910-5

First edition

© Text and layout SHEILA McCULLAGH MCMLXXXV
© In publication LADYBIRD BOOKS LTD MCMLXXXV

Tessa and the Magician

written by SHEILA McCULLAGH
illustrated by JOHN LOBBAN

This book belongs to:

_____

Ladybird Books Loughborough

Tessa Catchamouse was a very little cat,
with very big ears.

She lived in the garden of an old house.
A magician lived in the house.
Tessa lived in a hole under the steps
that led to the front door.
She lived there with her mother,
whose name was Pegs, and
her brother, whose name was Tim.

Tessa

One day, Tessa woke up very early
in the morning.
Her mother had gone out,
to look for food, and
her brother was still fast asleep.

Tessa woke up.

The old house had a big garden.

Nobody ever worked in the garden.

The grass grew long, and
the weeds grew wild.

It was a wonderful place to play in.

Tessa went out into the garden to play.

Tessa went out.

There was an old tree in the garden.
The old tree grew near the house.

Tessa ran over to the tree and
began to climb up it.
She climbed up the tree,
right up to the top.

the old tree

Tessa looked down from
the top of the tree.
The roof of the old house
was just below her.

Tessa looked down.

Tessa jumped down, on to the roof
of the old house.

Tessa jumped down.

She saw a window in the roof.

The window was open.

Tessa ran up to the window.

She looked down, into the room below.

Tessa looked down.

Tessa saw an old man in the room.
He was sitting in a chair, and
he was fast asleep.
He had long white hair, and
a long white beard.
"He must be the Magician,"
Tessa said to herself.

Tessa saw
the Magician.

A big wooden pole was propped up
near the window.
Tessa looked down at the pole.

"I think I could climb down that,"
she said to herself.
"The Magician is fast asleep,
and there are all kinds of
interesting things in that room."

She began to climb down the pole.

Magic Mice
rowing ears

Tessa looked down.

She hadn't gone very far,
when she found herself near a shelf.

Tessa jumped down, on to the shelf.
There was a jar on the shelf.
It was full of sugar mice.
There were white mice in the jar,
and they were all made out of sugar.
Tessa looked at the jar.
She was very hungry.

Tessa jumped down.

There was a label on the jar. It said:
"Magic Mice for growing ears."
Tessa couldn't read the label,
but she looked at the sugar mice,
and her mouth began to water.
She pushed the jar over.
The lid fell off, and
a white sugar mouse fell out.
Tessa ate the mouse.

It tasted very good.

Tessa ate the mouse.

She was just going to eat
another mouse, when she felt
a very funny feeling in her ears.

She put up a paw, to feel her ears.

Her ears were growing longer!

Tessa's ears
were growing longer.

"Miaow!" cried Tessa.

She was very frightened.
She felt her ears again with her paw.
Her ears were growing longer and longer!

Tessa's ears
were growing
longer and longer.

"Miaow!" cried Tessa. "Miaow! Miaow!"

She jumped down to the floor.
Tessa ran to the Magician.
Her ears were so big,
that she couldn't jump up,
so she climbed up the Magician's leg,
just as if she was climbing up a tree.

Tessa ran
to the Magician.

The Magician woke with a yell of pain.
He saw Tessa.

"Take your claws out of my leg!"
cried the Magician.
"Take your claws out of my leg!"

"Look at my ears!" cried Tessa.
"Look at my ears!
They won't stop growing!"

The Magician
saw Tessa.

The Magician began to laugh.

"You silly little cat," he said.
"You've been eating magic sugar mice.
You shouldn't do that.
They make your ears grow."

"**Please** stop my ears growing,"
cried Tessa.

The Magician laughed again.

"Mice, mice, go back in the jar.
Ears, ears, grow as short as you were,"
he cried.

And he snapped his fingers.

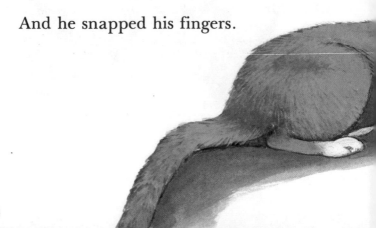

the Magician

At once, the jar righted itself.
All the white sugar mice flew back
into it.
Tessa's ears began to grow shorter.
They got shorter and shorter and shorter,
until they were just right.

"Oh, thank you!" cried Tessa.

She began to purr.

"That's all very well," said the Magician.
"But what about my poor leg?"

"I'm sorry about your leg," said Tessa.

Tessa and
the Magician

When Tessa got home again,
she told Pegs all about the Magician
and the sugar mice.

"You mustn't go and bother magicians,"
said her mother. "They can work magic."

"I know they can," said Tessa.
"But he's a very kind Magician, isn't he?"

Tessa and Pegs

Notes for the parent/teacher

When you have read the story, go back to the beginning. Look at each picture and talk about it, pointing to the caption below, and reading it aloud yourself.

Run your finger along under the words as you read, so that the child learns that reading goes from left to right. (You needn't say this in so many words. Children learn many useful things about reading by just reading with you, and it is often better to let them learn by experience, rather than by explanation.) When you next go through the book, encourage the child to read the words and sentences under the illustrations.

Mrs Pitter-Patter dropped the tail with a yell. She made such a noise, that she woke Mr Gotobed, who was fast asleep in bed in the house at the end of the lane.

Mr Gotobed woke up.

Don't rush in with the word before she* has time to think, but don't leave her floundering for too long. Always encourage her to feel that she is reading successfully, praising her when she does well, and avoiding criticism.

Now turn back to the beginning, and print the child's name in the space on the title page, using ordinary, not capital letters. Let her watch you print it: this is another useful experience.

*Children enjoy hearing the same story many times. Read this one as often as the child likes hearing it. The more opportunities she has of looking at the illustrations and **reading** the captions with you, the more she will come to recognise the words. Don't worry if she **remembers** rather than **reads** the captions. This is a normal stage in learning.*

If you have a number of books, let her choose which story she would like to have again.

**Footnote:* In order to avoid the continual "he or she", "him or her", the child is referred to in this book as "she". However, the stories are equally appropriate for boys and girls.

When you are sure that the child can read
these words successfully, ask her to
read them to you.

Tessa

Pegs

the Magician

There are more stories about Tessa and Tim and the Magician in these books:

Stage 1

the flying saucer

from Tim turns green